JAMES

Faith in Action

JAMES

Faith in Action

By

G. COLEMAN LUCK

MOODY PRESS • CHICAGO

Printed in the United States of America

CONTENTS

Chapter 1

FAITH TESTED

INTRODUCTION

ONE OF THE NEW TESTAMENT EPISTLES which is least known and studied by evangelical Christians is that of James. Great stress has been laid on the Pauline writings (and rightly so), but it should be remembered that the other New Testament books are likewise of real value. Indeed, it seems that James fills a pressing modern need more fully than does any other portion of the New Testament.

There has been some disparagement of James because of a misunderstanding of the true motive and purpose. It is well known that Luther considered it "an epistle of straw, and destitute of evangelic character." This is dangerous ground on which to stand. If one book of the Bible is to be rejected because of personal dislike and lack of understanding, where will the process end? The seed of later German ration-

7

alism is to be detected in this arbitrary statement of a great Christian who otherwise hon-
ored and exalted God's Word. Luther fancied
that he saw a conflict between James and Paul,
and in his zeal to exalt justification by faith
alone, he made this rash statement.

But rightly understood, it will be clearly seen
that there is not the shadow of a disagreement
between James and Paul. In the first place, the
Epistle of James, as scholars generally agree, is
probably the earliest book of the entire New
Testament, and was written some years before
Paul's great Epistle to the Romans. Thus it
could hardly be construed as an "answer" to
Paul's magnificent dissertation on justification
by faith.

In the second place, a careful study of this book
reveals that James is dealing with an entirely
different realm or aspect of the Christian life
from that which Paul emphasizes. Paul deals
primarily with the doctrine of *justification before God*, which comes not at all through works,
but entirely through faith in Christ and His
atoning death. James, on the other hand, is
dealing primarily with *justification before men*.
He is not disparaging a true heart faith, but
rather is emphasizing the fact that such a faith

should result in an outward life of piety and "good works." Only through these outward signs can men around us "see" our faith. In brief, James is dealing with the practical Christian life as it should be lived before the world—consequently his message is of perpetual importance.

The following cogent statement from Dr. D. A. Hayes in the *International Standard Bible Encyclopedia* well demonstrates the applicability of James to modern life:

> There are those who talk holiness and are hypocrites; those who make profession of perfect love and yet cannot live peaceably with their brethren; those who are full of pious phraseology but fail in practical philanthropy. This epistle was written for them. It may not give them much comfort, but it ought to give them much profit. The mysticism which contents itself with pious frames and phrases, and comes short in actual sacrifice and devoted service, will find its antidote here. The antinomianism that professes great confidence in free grace, but does not recognize the necessity for corresponding purity of life, needs to ponder the practical wisdom of this epistle.

The quietists who are satisfied to sit and sing themselves away to everlasting bliss ought to read this epistle until they catch its bugle note of inspiration to present activity and continuous good deeds. All who are long on theory and short on practice ought to steep themselves in the spirit of James; and since there are such people in every community and in every age, the message of the epistle will never grow old.

Dr. C. I. Scofield writes: "Perhaps there was never a time when the testimony of James, rightly understood, had a more necessary application than now."

THE HUMAN AUTHOR

James, the human author of this epistle, is an interesting though little known character of the New Testament. He should be carefully distinguished from several other men of the same name.

This James is called "the Lord's brother" by Paul (Gal. 1:19), being the son of Joseph and Mary, and thus, according to the flesh, a half brother of our Lord. In Matthew 13:55 he is mentioned first in a group of four brethren of Christ, and thus was apparently the eldest son of Joseph and Mary.

Before the death of Christ, he was apparently
not a believer in Jesus, for we are told in John
7:5 that "neither did his brethren believe in
him." After seeing the death and resurrection
of our Lord, however, he became a firm believer,
with the other brethren, and was a participant
in the prayer meeting which took place between
the ascension and Pentecost (Acts 1:14). He
soon rose to a place of prominence in the Jerusalem church, and at the time of the great
council of Acts 15 was the recognized leader of
that church. Paul speaks of him as a "pillar
of the church" and the director of its activities
(Gal. 2:9, 12).

James was a pious, devout man of sterling
Christian character, who truly lived the doctrine
he preached. Hegesippus (an early church historian who wrote about A.D. 175-189) speaks
of him in the highest terms, particularly as a
man of prayer. He says that James abstained
from wine and strong drink, as well as from
flesh, and that he lived a holy life. He alone
was permitted to enter the holy place in the
temple by the priests, and he was frequently
found there interceding for the people. He
prayed so much that his knees became hard
and calloused like a camel's knees. He was

faithful in the temple worship and had the confidence and respect of all the Jews, both Christians and non-Christians. It can easily be seen why he was called "James the Just."

Josephus (A.D. 37-95), the great Jewish historian, indicates that James was stoned to death at the order of the high priest, Ananus. This act brought a storm of protest from the most equitable citizens, so that Ananus was deposed after only three months in office. "There would seem to have been quite a widespread conviction among both the Christians and Jews that the afflictions which fell upon the holy city and the chosen people in the following years were in part a visitation because of the great crime of the murder of this just man" (Hayes, in the *International Standard Bible Encyclopedia*).

The details of James' martyrdom are supplied by Hegesippus, as quoted in the writings of Eusebius (A.D. 260-340). The scribes and Pharisees, after placing James on a pinnacle of the temple, begged him to restrain the people, as large numbers were embracing Christianity. "Tell us," they cried, "which is the door of Jesus?" (A taunting reference to James 5:8, 9, as much as to say: "By what door will he come when He returns?") James replied in a loud voice: "Why ask ye me concerning Jesus, the Son of Man? He sitteth at the right hand of power, and will come again on the clouds of heaven." Many of his hearers then cried: "Hosanna to the Son of David." This so infuriated the Pharisees that they threw him down headlong; then stoned him and beat him to death with a fuller's club. His dying words were: "Father, forgive them, for they know not what they do." Thus at his death he bore testimony to the precious truth of the second advent of Christ.

From this brief sketch it is easy to see that James exemplified in his life the teaching which he gave in his epistle concerning practical Christianity.

In the opening verses of his book James deals with the subject of "Faith Tested." Several tests of faith are to be found in chapter 1. The first of these, dealt with in the opening eight verses, shows that faith is tested by attitude toward trials from without.

The introduction in verse 1 is brief but noteworthy. Although "the Lord's brother" and the recognized leader of the Jerusalem church, James shows his true humility of spirit by calling himself simply "a servant of God and of the

Lord Jesus Christ." Far from arrogating any superior position to himself, he places himself on a level with all of God's servants.

To Whom Addressed

The epistle is directly addressed to "the twelve tribes which are scattered abroad," to whom James sends "greeting." As Paul's epistles were originally directed to some individual Christian, church, or group of churches, and through them to all, so James wrote originally to Jewish Christians scattered throughout the world. But the inspired truths of which he speaks are equally applicable to other Christians throughout this age.

It is of particular interest to note that James refers to the "twelve tribes." Some have imagined that certain tribes were lost at the time of the captivity, and so they speak of "ten lost tribes." Others have allowed their fancy to run so far afield as to imagine that the British people are the descendants of the "ten lost tribes," and thus all of English descent are identified as Israelites! The exponents of British Israelism seek to arrogate to themselves a position of superiority before God because of this supposed ancestry. Even if true, it would mean no superior position, for during the present age "both Jews and Gentiles . . . are all under sin" (Rom. 3:9) and can be saved only through faith in the Saviour.

However, the Bible speaks of no "lost tribes." All finally went into captivity, and later only a minority returned to rebuild Jerusalem under Ezra, Nehemiah, and Zerubbabel, but this minority contained members from each tribe. During New Testament times, the Israelites were still familiar with the tribes to which they belonged, but at the destruction of Jerusalem in A.D. 70 by Titus, all the official records were destroyed and the nation completely dispersed. In the ensuing confusion and persecution, tribal connections were eventually lost sight of and forgotten.

So today those whom we know as "Jews" are in reality representatives not only of Judah, but of all twelve tribes. Their tribal identity is unknown to themselves, but it is still known to God, as evidenced by the concise enumeration according to tribes of the Jewish remnant of the last days (Rev. 7:4-8).

PATIENCE THROUGH TRIAL

The text of James' letter begins with some rather unusual words: "My brethren, count it

all joy when ye fall into divers temptations"
(v. 2). Ordinarily we count it all joy when we
escape trials and temptations (for to such
James here refers). But we are told that, on the
contrary, we should rejoice when these trials
come.

The explanation is to be found in verse 3:
"Knowing this, that the trying of your faith
worketh patience." Here we see that faith is
presupposed by the writer, and external trials
which God sends are simply tests of this faith
within.

There is a most blessed thought here—God
is working in all the events of life, and through
each is seeking to mold Christian character, to
refine the gold from the dross. Therefore we
should rejoice in these trials because we can
know that God is dealing with us for our own
good.

In this dealing the particular thing He is
trying to perfect in us is *patience*. Patience is
usually thought of as calm resignation to God's
will in face of the inevitable. But Christian
patience, as spoken of in the New Testament, is
more than this. It is true that calm submission
is a part of it, but this is only the negative side.
On the positive side there is a steady and de-

termined perseverance, in spite of difficulties, toward the right—toward the goal of God's will for our lives.

This side of patience is expressed in the words of Paul: "I press toward the mark for the prize of the high calling of God in Christ Jesus" (Phil. 3:14). With such patience as this we can say: "For our light affliction, which is but for a moment, worketh for us a far more exceeding and eternal weight of glory; while we look not at the things which are seen, but at the things which are not seen: for the things which are seen are temporal; but the things which are not seen are eternal" (II Cor. 4:17, 18).

This patience may be compared to a person in a high wind. Just to stand upright, which is difficult, demonstrates the negative side of patience. But to press valiantly on in the face of the wind to some necessary goal demonstrates the positive side of patience.

This sort of patience is developed only through tribulation. A young minister once asked an older man of God to pray that he might have more patience, as he realized this was his great lack. The aged man knelt and began to pray that God would send trouble and difficulties upon the youth. Finally the younger brother tapped the older minister upon the shoulder, and whispered: "You must have misunderstood me; I asked that you would pray that I night have more patience, not more trouble." The answer was: "Remember, the Scripture says: 'Tribulation worketh patience' (Rom. 5:3). That is the only way!"

"But let patience have her perfect work, that ye may be perfect and entire, wanting nothing" (v. 4). Here it is evident, as already indicated, that the patience of James is an active virtue— it *works*. As these various trials come upon us we are to persevere in patience in order that its perfect work of refining may be wrought in our lives.

The goal of this patient endurance in testing is that all the rough edges of our character may be made smooth and that we may be complete in all the graces God wants us to have: "perfect and entire." *Entire* speaks of the possession of *all* these graces; *perfect* describes the measure of *each one*. God would have none·lacking or wanting in us.

GOD OFFERS WISDOM

But as we think of this picture of the complete Christian character, we cannot but realize that we yet fall woefully short, are indeed *lacking* in many ways. Chief of all perhaps is our lack of true wisdom to discern the divine dealings and profit by them. So James says: "If any of you lack wisdom, let him ask of God, that giveth to all men liberally, and upbraideth not; and it shall be given him" (v. 5).

God does not offer knowledge, for He expects us to obtain that through work and study, but He does offer *wisdom*. This is not just worldly astuteness, but rather divine wisdom, later described in 3:17. The way to receive this wisdom is simply *to ask*. God is waiting to supply our need; He is on "the giving hand"— the great Giver. He will give this wisdom "to all men," that is, to all who ask.

The description of the way in which He gives, is beautiful indeed. He gives *liberally*— with no thought of any return whatsoever. Many times when we give, we expect some sort of return. Not so with God.

Also He "upbraideth not." Blessed thought! Sometimes you have to upbraid those who ask you for gifts, and perhaps rightly so. You have to say: "What! are you coming to me again? What about that last gift I gave you? You showed no appreciation for it and did not put

it to proper use Go and use to good advantage
what I have already given before you come to
me again!" God might well speak in such
fashion to us, but we can be thankful that He
does not. "He upbraideth not."

THE UNWAVERING HEART

Once again in verse 6, James speaks of faith.
"But let him ask in faith, nothing wavering."
Faith is essential if we would receive the answer
to our prayers. "Without faith it is impossible
to please him: for he that cometh to God must
believe that he is, and that he is a rewarder of
them that diligently seek him" (Heb. 11:6).

If faith is lacking, and the heart is wavering
in unbelief, it is useless to ask anything of God.
Such a man James describes in the following
terms: "For he that wavereth is like a wave of
the sea driven with the wind and tossed. For
let not that man think that he shall receive
anything of the Lord. A double-minded man
is unstable in all his ways" (vv. 6-8).

Sometimes when a man is facing the tempests
of life he seeks God's aid and promises to follow
God's will if that aid is granted. Then when the
skies brighten, he immediately forgets God.
Such a man was Pharaoh of old. In the furnace

of affliction he promised to let the Israelites go
if God would grant relief. Then when the
plague was lifted, he forgot his promise. This
is what God calls a "double-minded man, unstable in all his ways." Such a man has little
claim upon God's promises. Instead, we are to
come with pure hearts of faith, assured that as
we are *single minded* in seeking His will, God
will graciously hear us.

Chapter 2

FAITH'S ATTITUDE TOWARD WORLDLY POSITION AND FLESHLY TEMPTATION

IN THE OPENING VERSES of the first chapter of his epistle, James shows that the attitude we take when faced by the trials and tribulations of life is a real test of the faith, or lack of faith, in our hearts. Then he proceeds to another test—our attitude toward the worldly position we occupy. He speaks of two extremes, poverty and wealth. How should the true Christian face either of these situations?

Poverty is dealt with in one verse: "Let the brother of low degree rejoice in that he is exalted" (1:9). In such a condition, instead of griping and complaining, "the brother"—the true Christian—should go on in fortitude and indeed *rejoice;* not in his poverty, but rather in his spiritual wealth in Christ. Let him remember that through faith he occupies the exalted position of a child of God, and that the heavenly

Father will "work all things together for good to them that love him."

The rich man, being perhaps more tempted to turn from God and trust in self, is given somewhat lengthier instruction. Being over-inclined to vain self-exaltation, he is admonished to consider the fact "that he is made low" (v. 10). He should always remember that God is no "respecter of persons" and that earthly riches are as nothing in His sight. The rich man is not to expect any preferential treatment, but must take his place with all other men as lost sinners saved only by divine grace. He can rejoice in the fact that he is thus brought low in order that he may receive salvation through faith in Christ even as others.

Lest he should be inclined to forget this, he should consider the transitoriness of his own life and wealth. James compares the rich man with "the flower of the grass," which soon passes away. He is like the beautiful flower of the field, fresh in the summer morning, but withered and gone by nightfall because of the burning heat of the sun. "So also shall the rich man fade away in his ways." How clearly this same thought is advanced by our Lord in His parable of the rich fool, a man who trusted in his riches rather than in God, and who soon "faded away in his ways!"

Beginning with verse 12, the writer again uses the word "temptation," but this time in an entirely different sense from that of verse 2. There temptations referred to trials and tribulations which come upon one from without, often quite unexpectedly. Here he uses the word temptation to refer rather to solicitation to evil. Both of these uses of this word in the New Testament must be recognized and understood.

"Blessed is the man that endureth temptation: for when he is tried, he shall receive the crown of life, which the Lord hath promised to them that love him" (v. 12). The man who successfully endures such solicitation to evil is pronounced "blessed" or "happy." By turning from such temptation he has demonstrated by his purity of life that he really loves God, therefore he is promised "the crown of life" with which God will some day reward all those who have truly loved Him.

Joseph's Example

An eminent example of this is to be found in the life of Joseph. He resisted the evil solicitation of Potiphar's wife, even though it meant years of unjust imprisonment. By his purity of life, even in the face of this terrible temptation, he demonstrated that he truly loved God, and thus showed his inward faith by his outward actions.

While temptation in the sense of trials and tribulations is sent from God for a definite purpose in our lives, we are not to think of temptation in the sense of solicitation to evil as coming from God. "Let no man say when he is tempted, I am tempted of God: for God cannot be tempted with evil, neither tempteth he any man: but every man is tempted, when he is drawn away of his own lust, and enticed" (vv. 13, 14).

During recent years, on certain occasions plain clothes policemen solicited merchants to infringe on O.P.A. regulations, in order that when they yielded and broke the law cases might be made against them. God is not to be thought of as stooping to such tactics. When a man commits sin and iniquity, he cannot blame God by saying that he has merely yielded to the temptation God sent.

James makes it clear that God can neither Himself be tempted in such a way, nor does He tempt others to commit sin. Such temptation comes rather from the corrupt, sin nature

within man himself. These evil lusts and passions are within us all. Other persons no doubt
have a part in such temptation, but it is the sin
nature within that responds; and when a man
falls he can in the final analysis blame no one
but himself.

Progress of Sin

Lest any should minimize sin, as some nowa-
days are inclined to do, verse 15 contains a
terrible warning as to sin and its final result.
Three simple steps are traced: lust, sin, death.
First there is the evil desire in the heart. If
encouraged, this gives birth to open and flagrant
sin, and sin in turn eventually produces death.
In the case of unbelievers, this death will be
eternal death. If unconfessed and unrepented
of in the life of the believer, it will eventually
result in physical death.

John speaks of this when he mentions "a sin
unto death" (I John 5:16). Paul states with
regard to certain sins that "for this cause many
are weak, and sickly among you, and many
sleep" (I Cor. 11:30). When a believer dies
it means either that the life work assigned to
him by the Lord has been completed, or that he
has gone so far out of the will of the Lord that
his testimony is ruined and the Lord must call

home His erring child. "Do not err, my beloved brethren." Let us be careful to distinguish these important things.

FATHER OF LIGHTS

So far from attributing *evil* to God, on the contrary, let us realize that our heavenly Father sends only *good things* to us. Everything good proceeds from Him. "Every good gift, and every perfect gift is from above, and cometh down from the Father of lights, with whom is no variableness, neither shadow of turning" (v. 17).

Once again we have the giving God called to our attention. He is called "the Father of lights," perhaps an allusion to God as Creator of the marvelous heavenly lights. *Light* speaks of purity and holiness, and these heavenly bodies, brilliant and wonderful as they are, but feebly represent the glorious light of the great Creator Himself.

But these physical lights are subject to alternations of light and darkness. Even the shining sun has its "spots." But there are no spots—no variableness—within the perfect light of the great Creator. " 'Shadow of turning'—the *shadow mark* cast *from* a heavenly body in its *turning* or revolution, e.g., when the moon is eclipsed by the earth, and the sun by the moon" (Fausset). Even the greatest of created things may change, but God never.

"Of his own will begat he us with the word of truth, that we should be a kind of first fruits of his creatures" (v. 18). Here James points us to the greatest gift of all: the fact that this sovereign and omnipotent God of His own free will chose us to be heirs of eternal life through faith in His Son. He confirmed this choice by sending us the gospel of His dear Son —"the word of truth"; and when we believed it, He regenerated us—we were born again.

What was God's purpose in so dealing with us? "That we should be a kind of first fruits of his creatures." We are "created in Christ Jesus unto good works, which God hath before ordained that we should walk in them" (Eph. 2:10).

The first sheaf of the new crop, together with a sacrifice, was presented in the Levitical ceremony in the temple on the day after the Passover Sabbath. By this, acknowledgment was made that all came from God and belonged to Him, and none was to be used for food until this ceremony had been performed.

The first fruits were also a sample or specimen of the bounteous harvest of golden grain which would eventually follow. Christ is "the first fruits of them that slept." In His resurrection we see a wonderful specimen of what God will eventually do for all believers.

While the Lord is the true fulfillment of the first fruits, James says that we too are "*a kind* of first fruits." In other words, God is seeking to perfect Christian character in us now in order that we may be specimens, if you please, of what He wants humanity to be, and as samples of what He, through the gospel of Christ, is able to make of ordinary human beings.

Once again we come back to James' great theme of the practical Christian life, lived before men. Is your life such a manifestation of God's grace that men, seeing you, desire to know your Saviour also and to experience His life-changing work?

Chapter 3

DOERS OF THE WORD

"PAUL IS A PREACHER OF FAITH, but of faith which works by love. James is the preacher of works, but of works which are the fruit of faith" (Alexander Maclaren).

In the first chapter of his epistle, James mentions a number of things which test faith, but the supreme test of all is that of obedience to God's revealed Word. This is made very clear in James 1:19-27.

HEARERS OF THE WORD

First, James speaks of *receiving* the Word (vv. 19-21). He writes in verse 19: "Wherefore, my beloved brethren, let every man be swift to hear, slow to speak, slow to wrath." It should be observed that the person who has true faith in Christ is enjoined to be *swift* to do one thing and *slow* to do two others.

In the first place, the Christian should be *swift to hear*. Even worldly-wise people recog-

nize the value of such action. The following
is a very familiar little jingle along this line:

> A wise old owl lived in an oak.
> The more he knew, the less he spoke;
> The less he spoke, the more he knew;
> And this same thing applies to you.

Remember that when you *speak* you are
not learning anything new, but simply repeat-
ing that which you already know.

But the special injunction of James is that
the man of faith should be swift to hear "the
word of truth," which was just mentioned in
the preceding verse (v. 18).

As to being slow in speech and wrath, Dr.
Charles R. Erdman has well said: "Let him
[that is, the one who has faith] be 'slow to
speak,' humbly taking the place of a learner;
or if it becomes his duty to testify or to teach,
let him do so in modesty and reverence, avoid-
ing all carelessness and flippancy, and self-
confidence. Let him also be slow to wrath.
Unhappily, religious discussions are too often
attended with heat and anger. Too many public teachers seem to feel that the bitterness with
which they assail their opponents will attest
their zeal and devotion."

Such an attitude as this is far from the truth. James states very clearly that "the wrath of man worketh not the righteousness of God" (v. 20). Anger and bitterness will not produce the patient endurance God is seeking to work out in our lives. "Wherefore" (we are told in v. 21) we should "lay apart" two things—*all filthiness* and *superfluity of naughtiness.*

The word *filthiness* speaks of vile lusts and evil passions. You would not think of clothing the outer man with garments that were covered with the vilest kind of filth. Then how much more should you lay aside such garments in connection with the inner man—the soul—the real you!

The old English expression *superfluity of naughtiness* is translated in the American Revised Version "overflowing of wickedness." The thought here is of spiritual wickedness, such as malice or hatred, which overflows from our beings.

If we want to demonstrate our faith, let us turn from these things and instead, "receive with meekness the engrafted word, which is able to save your souls" (v. 21b). God's Word is spoken of as "the engrafted word," that is, it is a *living word,* and when received, becomes a vital part of our very beings.

Further, it is a *powerful word*—it is able to save the soul. When a person receives and believes God's Word, the gospel message, then his soul is saved. "For the word of God is quick, and powerful, and sharper than any two-edged sword, piercing even to the dividing asunder of soul and spirit, and of joints and marrow, and is a discerner of the thoughts and intents of the heart" (Heb. 4:12).

So the substance of James' teaching in this section is that the one who truly has faith in Christ will be eager to hear God's Word, and will, turning away from evil, receive it with meekness.

Lest any, however, should misunderstand, James makes it very clear that hearing God's Word alone will bring no blessing (vv. 22-27). The man who has real faith in his heart will not only listen to God's Word, but he will put it into effect in his own life.

DOERS OF THE WORD

James says: "But be ye doers of the word, and not hearers only, deceiving your own selves. For if any be a hearer of the word, and not a doer, he is like unto a man beholding his natural face in a glass: for he beholdeth himself, and goeth his way, and straightway forgetteth what manner of man he was" (vv. 22-24).

If a person hears God's Word without putting it into practice in his own life, then he deceives himself if he thinks he derives any benefit from it. "It is not enough to remember what we hear, and to be able to repeat it, and to give testimony to it, and commend it and write it, and preserve what we have written; that which all this is in order to, and which crowns the rest, is that we be doers of the Word" (Matthew Henry).

James uses a very striking illustration in verses 23 and 24. The person who thinks he derives benefit from hearing God's Word, even though he refuses to put it into practice in his life, is like a man who beholds his face in a looking glass, then turns away and forgets what he saw.

When I arose this morning, one of the first things I did was go into the bathroom and look into the mirror. There I saw a tousled head of hair, eyes filled with sleep, and an ugly stubble of beard. Did I then dress and leave for my work, thinking that I was ready for the day because I had peered into the mirror? By no means. If so, I would have been deceiving myself. After one look, I proceeded to comb and brush my hair, shave my face, apply soap and water and in every way attempt to make myself presentable. The mirror showed what was wrong, but before I could receive any benefit from that knowledge, I had to apply what I had learned to my own life.

Thus it is with one who reads or hears God's Word and notes therein his spiritual condition, and then fails to do anything about it. No, this is not the way to get blessing from God's Word. The true way—the way of faith—is described in verse 25. "But whoso looketh into the perfect law of liberty, and continueth therein, he being not a forgetful hearer, but a doer of the work, this man shall be blessed in his deed."

Instruction for the Christian life, the life believers are to live under the present dispensation of grace, is here called "the perfect law of liberty." Unlike the Old Testament law, which was "weak through the flesh" (Rom. 8:3), this New Testament instruction is perfect. In other words, the Mosaic law commanded, but it gave no power to the person to obey the command. Now, however, when we believe on Christ, God sends the Holy Spirit into our hearts to enable us to do those things which are pleasing to Him.

The Old Testament law was a law of bondage. It said, "This do, and thou shalt live." The teachings of grace are just the opposite; they are the law of liberty. Christ says, "If ye love me, keep my commandments." Now He puts His law into our hearts (Heb. 8:10), so that we will delight through the power of the Holy Spirit to do His will. Then we have true blessing.

The last two verses of chapter 1 contain two practical examples of what James is talking about. An example not to imitate is shown in verse 26, and then, contrasting, one to imitate in verse 27.

"If any man among you seem to be religious, and bridleth not his tongue, but deceiveth his own heart, this man's religion is vain." Here is a striking example of one who is a hearer but not a doer of the Word. Three things are said about this hypothetical person. First, he *seems* to be religious, or, literally, "thinks himself" to be religious. Second, he does not "bridle" his tongue. Third, he deceives his own heart.

OUTWARD RELIGION

The word *religion* is a broad term and little

used in the New Testament. In fact, it is used only five times and the word *religious* is used but twice. It means simply "belief in the supernatural and the expression of that belief," and so can apply to any system of worship from Christianity to the crudest idolatry.

Here, when James refers to a man being *religious,* he refers to outward, external ceremonials or rituals, which a man performs in order to be pleasing to God—what we might call today *public worship.* The picture is that of a man who goes through various forms and ceremonies of worship, and is therefore thought to be, indeed *thinks himself* to be, a very religious man. But what do we find when we examine his life? It shows no evidence of regeneration, no sign of any inward change. His religion is all on the outside.

James mentions just one item to prove this. The man in question fails to bridle his tongue. He has an evil, bitter tongue that produces vile language, backbiting, and slandering of others, while praising himself. "Out of the abundance of the heart the mouth speaketh" (Matt. 12:34). By his very conversation this man shows that he cares nothing for God and His will.

The third thing that James says about such

a one is very terrible: he "deceiveth his own heart." It is possible for one to be lost and headed for Hell and yet to hypnotize himself into thinking that all is well. Remember the words of our blessed Saviour: "Except a man be born again, he cannot see the kingdom of God" (John 3:3). Alexander Maclaren's words are startling, but true: "There will be plenty of orthodox Christians and theological professors and students who will find themselves, to their very great surprise, amongst the goats at last."

What is James' verdict about the man who has such a religion—very punctilious in observing rituals and ceremonies of worship, but demonstrating by his very words that he has no inward renewing of the heart, no regeneration? He simply says, "This man's religion is vain." It is an empty, futile thing. It is possible to be very religious and yet unsaved (see Rom. 10:1, 2).

LIVING FAITH IN EVIDENCE

Verse 27 contains the contrast: "Pure religion and undefiled before God and the Father is this, To visit the fatherless and widows in their affliction, and to keep himself unspotted from the world." Here is the pure and undefiled form of religion—the true way in which to show that we do have a living faith in God our heavenly Father. This can be done by our actions toward others, and by living personal lives of godliness.

With regard to others, James of course does not mean to give an exhaustive list when he mentions *orphans* and *widows*. These are merely examples of people manifestly in need. Neither does he mean by *visit* simply making a social call, though this may sometimes be a true service to the Lord. In short, James is speaking of *helping others*, that is, of showing real concern for those in need. If this is done through love for God, it is acceptable worship.

Beyond this, we can show our faith not only by loving service to others, but also by seeking through His grace to live personal lives of purity and godliness. We live in a sinful world. It is hard to live in it without becoming soiled and contaminated, but the true man of faith will seek to keep himself "unspotted from the world." The apostle John tells what is in the world—the lust of the flesh (that is, bodily passion), the lust of the eyes (that is, mental passion), and the pride of life (jealousy and rivalry) (I John 2:16). To keep oneself from these is to keep unspotted from the world.

Let no one forget that such a life as this must be built on a solid foundation. It has been well said, "Begin with Jesus Christ and the wish to please Him, and there is the root out of which all these graces and beauties will most surely come."

Chapter 4

JUDGED BY THE LAW OF LIBERTY

So far as salvation is concerned, true believers in Christ will never have to face judgment. God's Word makes this very clear. "Verily, verily, I say unto you, He that heareth my word, and believeth him that sent me, hath eternal life, and cometh not into judgment, but hath passed out of death into life" (John 5:24, R.V.). "There is therefore now no condemnation to them that are in Christ Jesus" (Rom. 8:1, R.V.). Christ has borne the penalty of our sins on the cross, and if we receive Him as Saviour, then the guilt of sin is dealt with once for all.

This great truth, however, should not be allowed to obscure the tremendous fact that Christians *will* have their *deeds* judged. "For we must all appear before the judgment seat of Christ; that every one may receive the things done in his body, according to that he hath done, whether it be good or bad" (II Cor. 5:10).

In his great epistle concerning the practical
Christian life, James speaks of this judgment
and says that we should ever live in the light
of it (2:12). In the first thirteen verses of his
second chapter he deals in a vivid manner with
the question of our attitude toward others as
being a true test of faith, and something that
will have to be answered for before the judgment seat of Christ.

Christian Faith Defined

This important chapter opens with a command. "My brethren, have not the faith of our
Lord Jesus Christ, the Lord of glory, with respect of persons." By way of introduction to the
main subject it should be noted in this verse
that *Christian* faith is *faith in the Lord Jesus
Christ.*

James, writing under the Holy Spirit's inspiration, uses the full title of our Lord. Remember
the significance of each name. *Lord* is the New
Testament word corresponding with the Old
Testament *Jehovah.* It speaks of the deity and
authority of our Saviour. *Jesus* reveals His humanity and saviourhood. *Christ* is the Greek
word corresponding to the Hebrew *Messiah,*
the *Anointed One.* It is the official title of our
Lord. In Old Testament times men were

anointed for three offices—prophet, priest and king. Christ combines all three of these offices in His one perfect Person. He is *the* Prophet, Priest and King—God's Anointed One.

In the expression, "the Lord of glory," the words *the Lord,* in our Authorized Version, are in italics, indicating that the phrase was not in the original but was added by the translators to complete, as they thought, the sense. Here, however, the statement becomes more striking if these extra words are omitted.

In this verse, therefore, Christ is simply called *the glory.* Thus James refers to the Shekinah glory, which was the outward manifestation of God's presence in the temple of old. Christ Himself is the Shekinah glory of God tabernacling in flesh. "And the Word became flesh, and tabernacled among us" (John 1:14, R.V. margin).

So then *Christian* faith is faith in a Person who is both human and divine, a Saviour who is Prophet, Priest and King, truly Immanuel, "God with us." Anything less does not deserve the name *Christian.*

TRUTHS APPLIED

But observe that James makes a very practical application of these great doctrinal truths. He

says that those who have faith in such a Person—
who loved *all* and gave Himself for *all*—should
not practice "respect of persons." Indeed let us
say *must* not, for it is a command that James
gives.

What is the meaning of "respect of persons"?
Making unfair distinctions between people, or
judging by outward appearances alone. The
first two words of the verse add great weight
to the command: "my brethren." If we are
brethren we are equal before the Lord. He is
no respecter of persons.

Verses 2-4 present a very graphic illustration
of the wrong attitude in this matter. "For if
there come unto your assembly a man with a
gold ring, in goodly apparel, and there come in
also a poor man in vile raiment; and ye have
respect to him that weareth the gay clothing,
and say unto him, Sit thou here in a good place;
and say to the poor, Stand thou there, or sit
here under my footstool: are ye not then partial
in yourselves, and are become judges of evil
thoughts?"

In these verses James probably refers to an
incident that he had recently witnessed, an
actual example of what he is talking about.
Here is the picture: A group of people are as-

sembled for public worship. Two strangers come in. One is richly dressed. His apparel is described as "goodly" (v. 2) and even "gay" (v. 3). On his finger is an ornate gold ring. He seems to be a man of wealth and social position. The second man, on the contrary, is poorly dressed. He is evidently a laboring man, for his clothes are worn and soiled. What happens? The rich man is ushered to one of the best seats and is told: "Sit thou here in a good place." The poor man is told to stand or to sit on the floor in some inconspicuous place. (Notice, by the way, that the usher not only has a chair, but also a "footstool!")

Now what does this mean? Those guilty of such deeds have become "partial" and "judges with evil thoughts." By their actions they have said that the soul of the rich man is very valuable, while that of the poor man is worth little. How false this is! In God's sight both are equally precious. This same attitude is to be found in many churches and among many Christians today. Further illustrations are needless.

A Foolish Attitude

Verses 5-7 provide a divine commentary on the foolishness of such an attitude. "Hearken, my beloved brethren, Hath not God chosen the poor of this world rich in faith, and heirs of the kingdom which he hath promised to them that love him? But ye have despised the poor. Do not rich men oppress you, and draw you before the judgment seats? Do not they blaspheme that worthy name by the which ye are called?"

How unreasonable is respect of persons! After all, a person may be poor in this world's goods and yet rich in the eyes of God. As a matter of fact, James says, as we examine those who in the past have shown themselves "rich in faith," in the great majority of instances have they not been people who had very little earthly wealth? Of course not always—thank God for some exceptions to this rule. Lady Huntingdon, the gospel-loving friend of the Wesleys, used to say that she was saved by an "m," for, said she, if I Corinthians 1:26 had read "not any wise, not any noble are called," then she would not have been saved. But it does not read "not *any*," but "not *many*."

It is indeed true that the rich can be saved as well as the poor through faith in Christ, but it is very easy for a man with wealth to depend on his riches rather than on the Lord. This is doubtless what our Lord referred to in His comment on the rich young ruler (Luke 18:24, 25).

But in spite of this fact, many who profess the name of Christ "despise the poor." James further scores such an attitude by showing that often the rich are very disagreeable to get along with, and even oppress the poor. Some hate the very name of Christ. Why then toady to them? Remember, however, that it is not a question of favoring the poor and being rude to the rich. The point is that equal love and kindness should be shown to all, by those who have real faith in the Lord Jesus Christ.

Why, James goes on to say, the true attitude is shown even in the Old Testament. "If ye fulfill the royal law according to the scripture, Thou shalt love thy neighbor as thyself, ye do well" (v. 8). In the synagogues of James' day, it was customary for distinctions to be shown, after the above described manner, in the seating, different trades having their separate sections. But this was certainly not according even to the Old Testament revelation.

James quotes from Leviticus 19:18 what he calls the "royal law" (*royal* because it is the king of all laws, the summing up of all the laws pertaining to man's relation to man): "Thou

shalt love thy neighbor as thyself." If any wish
to quibble as to who is one's neighbor, the
answer our Lord Jesus gave to a certain law-
yer is very clear. In His parable of the Good
Samaritan, He showed plainly that there is no
distinction—all are neighbors, and we are not
only to be just as concerned about others as
about ourselves, but to be equally concerned
for all. To fulfill such a law is indeed to "do
well."

Not only is the proper attitude shown in
the Old Testament, but *respect of persons* is
definitely against Old Testament law. "But if ye
have respect to persons, ye commit sin, and are
convinced of the law as transgressors. For,
whosoever shall keep the whole law, and yet
offend in one point, he is guilty of all. For he
that said, Do not commit adultery, said also,
Do not kill. Now if thou commit no adultery,
yet if thou kill, thou art become a transgressor
of the law" (vv. 9-11).

Condemned a Sin

James has previously shown that respect of
persons, making unfair distinctions because of
prejudice, is *unreasonable*. Now he states that
it is positively *sinful*. If we were living in the
age of law—the Old Testament Mosaic dispen-

sation—and did such things, we would be law-breakers. And, further, such action would make us guilty of breaking "the whole law."

Let it be carefully observed that James says, "Whosoever shall keep the whole law, and yet offend in one point, he is guilty of all" (v. 10). Some readers may think this is harsh and unfair. Mr. Moody used the illustration of a man held suspended over a cliff by a chain of ten links. What happens if all ten links are broken? The man falls to his doom. What happens if just one link is broken? The man falls just the same. How many lies does it take to make a liar? Just one. How many thefts to make a thief? Just one. How many murders to make a murderer? Just one. How many laws must be broken before a man becomes a law-breaker? Just one. Let those who rely upon their own good works to save them, take this verse to heart.

But the principle point James is driving home is that the one who shows "respect of persons" is a lawbreaker and "guilty of all."

However, we who belong to Christ are "not under law but under grace," as the apostle Paul informs us (Rom. 6:14). Does this mean, then, that Christians are "lawless," that it matters

little how we behave? Not at all. There is
coming a time when we must all give an account of our actions before the judgment seat
of Christ. James says that we should keep this
constantly in mind. "So speak ye, and so do,
as they that shall be judged by the law of liberty.
For he shall have judgment without mercy, that
hath showed no mercy; and mercy rejoiceth
against judgment" (vv. 12, 13).

As we speak, as we act, let us remember that
we must some day answer for these things—
we must some day be judged by the "law of
liberty." The Old Testament law was a "law
of bondage." The precepts of our law—the
Christian's rule of life—make it a "law of
liberty."

Why is it called a law of *liberty?* Because it
commands the things that we delight to do
if we are truly born again through faith in Him.
Remember the stirring words of the apostle:
according to the grace of God which is given
unto me, as a wise masterbuilder, I have laid
the foundation, and another buildeth thereon.
But let every man take heed how he buildeth
thereupon. For other foundation can no man
lay than that is laid, which is Jesus Christ. Now
if any man build upon this foundation gold,

silver, precious stones, wood, hay, stubble; every man's work shall be made manifest: for the day shall declare it, because it shall be revealed by fire; and the fire shall try every man's work of what sort it is. If any man's work abide which he hath built thereupon, he shall receive a reward. If any man's work shall be burned, he shall suffer loss: but he himself shall be saved; yet so as by fire" (I Cor. 3:10-15).

James closes this passage with a reiteration of his constant theme: that outward actions show very clearly what is on the inside of a man. The one who is implacable, who shows no mercy to his fellow men, demonstrates clearly that he knows nothing of real faith, regardless of his profession. Such a one will some day have "judgment without mercy," says the apostle. The one who truly trusts Christ will be kind and merciful to others, and in the day of God's wrath, he will indeed obtain mercy himself, for "mercy rejoiceth against judgment."

Chapter 5

FAITH THAT CANNOT SAVE

THE LAST HALF of James 2 should be examined with extreme care, since it is this section that has caused some people to feel that James contradicts the apostle Paul. In this connection let us heed the admonition: "Study to show thyself approved unto God, a workman that needeth not to be ashamed, rightly dividing the word of truth" (II Tim. 2:15). Of one thing we can be sure—the Holy Spirit, the real author of the epistles by both Paul and James, does not contradict Himself. So any interpretation which would seem to make Him do so indicates a failure to "rightly divide" the Scriptures.

A thoughtful consideration of these verses will immediately reveal that they do not repudiate salvation by faith in Christ. Indeed they exalt true faith. There is a so-called faith that is really not *faith* at all, just as there is a gospel which is not *the* gospel (Gal. 1:6, 7). This

spurious faith which is really not *faith* at all
we may indeed call a "faith that cannot save."
This is what James rejects.

PROFESSION ONLY

James 2:14-26 gives a careful description of
this "faith that cannot save." We are told that
it is *dead faith*, that it is *without works,* that it
is mere *intellectual* assent to the truth (vv.
14-20).

To be more specific, James says that *it is all
profession:* "What doth it profit, my brethren,
though a man say he hath faith, and have not
works? can faith save him? If a brother or sister
be naked and destitute of daily food, and one
of you say unto them, Depart in peace, be ye
warmed and filled; notwithstanding ye give
them not those things which are needful to the
body; what doth it profit?" (vv. 14-16).

Verse 14 should be noted particularly. The
emphasis is on the word *say.* What doth it
profit if a man *say* he hath faith, and have not
works? It is true that, as far as service for God
goes, a man's limbs may be paralyzed without
his tongue being affected. James pictures a man
who boasts and brags about the faith he pos-
sesses, yet when his life is examined, it is clearly
seen that there is not one indication that he

is truly a child of God. He has no "works." This demonstrates very plainly that his "faith" (if you want to call it that) is just a matter of words and nothing more. If a man has real faith in God—in Christ—it is *bound* to make a difference in his life.

This is not to say that unless a man is absolutely perfect he is not saved. Not at all. None of us is absolutely perfect; we are not talking about sinless perfection. But it *is* to say that if a person takes Jesus Christ as Saviour in sincerity—if the risen Christ comes to dwell in the *heart*—there is of necessity a change in the *life*. If a man makes a profession of faith but his life remains absolutely unchanged, we can well ask with James, "Can *that* faith save him?" (as the R.V. correctly renders the last part of v. 14). Of course *real* faith can save him. But "can *that* faith save him?"—that is, can he be saved by faith that is all profession, a matter of mere words and nothing more?

To illustrate, James again uses a vivid experience. He speaks of an affluent person commiserating with a poverty-stricken brother or sister who actually lacks the essentials of life. The fact that this prosperous one expresses a desire to see the other clothed and fed, but does not give any material aid though well able to do so, shows that his concern is not real, but merely a matter of hypocritical words. As the old saying goes, "Actions speak louder than words."

This dead faith of which James speaks, this faith that cannot save, not only is all profession and no possession, but is *lifeless*. "Even so faith, if it hath not works, is dead, being alone" (v. 17). Real faith is a living, vital thing. It is the soul reaching out and taking hold of the promises of God.

But this false faith of which James speaks is like a corpse. A corpse looks like a man and yet it is only a lump of clay, because it lacks the one vital essential—*life*. So this faith which is all profession may look to the careless observer like the real thing; however, it is not real, but lifeless—*dead*—"being alone" (literally, by itself). It is like a body without a soul.

Further, we see that *it is contrasted with real faith*. "Yea, a man may say, Thou hast faith, and I have works: show me thy faith without thy works, and I will show thee my faith by my works."

Observe carefully what James is *not* saying in this verse. He is *not* talking about two men one of whom has *faith* and no *works*, and the other of whom has *works* and no *faith*. A thousand times no!

Both of the men referred to in this verse *claim* to have *faith*. But one cannot substantiate his claim. He *says* he has faith, but his life shows no evidence of any work of grace. The other man likewise claims to have faith, and to prove it he says, "Look at my life and see that a change has taken place. Look at my *works*— look at the things I have done since I made profession of faith in Christ; look at the life I have lived, and you can see that something real has taken place in my heart. You can't see my faith—that is inside my heart. But you can see my *works,* and by those works I can show you the unseen faith which motivated them."

O reader, can men see your faith shining out in the life that you live? If not, ask yourself seriously if *you* have ever had a real transaction with the Lord, if you have ever taken Jesus Christ as *your own Saviour.* Have *you* been born again?

The sham faith which James calls "dead faith" is said also to be similar to the belief of the demons. "Thou believest that there is one God; thou doest well: the devils also believe, and tremble" (v. 19).

This is a continuation of the illustration referred to in the verse just preceding. The man who claims to have faith but gives no evidence of it in his life apparently seeks to defend himself by saying that he *does* indeed have faith, that he believes in one God. Whereupon the other man says in effect: "Oh, so you believe in one God; that is very well and good. But simply to believe in the fact of the *existence* of God is *not* saving faith. Why the demons themselves believe this! They firmly believe in the existence of Almighty God. And that belief has more of an effect on *them* than it has on *you*, for they tremble or shudder when they think of it. But there is no question of them having saving faith. They believe in the existence of God, but at the same time hate and bitterly oppose that God."

Knowing the facts about God as revealed in the Bible is one thing; trusting in Him and depending on His Son Jesus Christ for salvation is quite another. We need to know the facts and accept the truthfulness of these facts, but that is only preparation. This is valueless unless it is followed by true faith which claims the promises of God and demonstrates itself by a changed life.

As a final description James indicates that this
dead faith is *fruitless.* "But wilt thou know,
O vain man, that faith without works is dead
[literally *barren*]?" (v. 20). "Wilt thou know"
—sad to say there are many vain, foolish people
who do *not* want to know these facts from
God's Word, indeed, *will* not know. They
prefer to live in a fool's paradise, so to speak,
and to pride themselves on their faith and
religion, when they really know nothing
whatever of saving faith. This kind of faith
which is only an empty acknowledgment of certain facts about God is *barren*—produces nothing
—does not result in salvation. It is not at all
what the apostle Paul was speaking of when he
stated that a man is justified by faith.

REAL FAITH—ABRAHAM

To close his discussion of this faith that cannot save, James turns to two practical examples
of real faith as found in the Old Testament. He
brings out very clearly just how these cases differ
from the dead faith of which he was just speaking.

The first of these great examples is that of
Abraham. "Was not Abraham our father justified by works, when he had offered Isaac his son
upon the altar? Seest thou how faith wrought

with his works, and by works was faith made perfect? And the Scripture was fulfilled which saith, Abraham believed God, and it was imputed unto him for righteousness: and he was called the Friend of God. Ye see then how that by works a man is justified, and not by faith only."

These words may seem, when considered superficially, to contradict those of the apostle Paul as found in Romans 4:1-3. But a little consideration will show that James is discussing a different side of the question. Paul shows that so far as his standing *before God* was concerned, Abraham was not justified (declared righteous) because of his works, for he was a sinful man as all the rest of us. But he believed God, and his faith was counted for righteousness. He stepped out in trustful dependence on the promises of God even when they seemed contrary to human possibility, and thus exercised saving faith. In this way he was justified before God.

James, on the other hand, once again speaks of works as manifesting to men the inward faith which cannot otherwise be observed. When Abraham, at the command of God, took his beloved son Isaac and prepared to offer him as a sacrifice, then all men could see by this tre-

mendous act of works what a sublime faith in
God he really had. Thus was he "justified by
works." That is, he was declared righteous *before men* by this act which proceeded from his
inward faith. Thus "faith wrought with his
works"—faith showed itself real by producing
works, and we are told that his faith was made
perfect by works. When a tree comes to maturity
and produces fruit, then by its fruit is the tree
made perfect.

So James says that the Scripture statement,
made some years before the offering of Isaac,
"Abraham believed God, and it was imputed to
him for righteousness," was fulfilled. As one
writer points out, this statement implies, "not
only that the root of the sacrifice was faith, but
that the words were true in a yet higher sense
and completer degree, when that sacrifice had
'perfected' the patriarch's faith."

Abraham is called by a beautiful title, "the
friend of God" (see II Chron. 20:7; Isa. 41:8).
This is the title by which the Moslems yet love
to speak of him. Dr. Maclaren, in a sermon on
this text, itemizes five characteristics of friendship, true both on a human level and with regard to our relationship to God.

(1) Friends trust and love one another; (2)

friends have frank and familiar intercourse with one another; (3) friends delight to meet each other's wishes; (4) friends give gifts to each other; (5) friends stand up for each other.

The other example from the Old Testament is that of a woman, and what a contrast to Abraham she provides! "Likewise also was not Rahab the harlot justified by works, when she had received the messengers, and had sent them out another way? For as the body without the spirit is dead, so faith without works is dead also" (vv. 25, 26).

REAL FAITH—RAHAB

Rahab (whose story is found in Josh. 2 and 6) was not a member of the chosen nation. Instead, she was a heathen woman, apparently of loose moral character formerly. But she placed her trust in Jehovah and believed that He would fulfill His promises to Israel. Therefore, when the Israelite spies came to her city of Jericho, she befriended and protected them, because she wanted to be on God's side. By these acts she showed that she did have a real living faith. in Him. So she too is said by James to be "justified by works," that is, her actions showed to men that she was indeed one of God's own.

The discussion is concluded by the statement

that faith (so-called) which produces no works, no outward manifestation, is like a corpse, lifeless and dead, and therefore worthless.

This word of personal application: It is well for us sometimes to examine our own experience to see if we have ever exercised real faith in Christ. Is our experience merely that we have answered "yes" to some questions asked us and joined a church? If so, let us turn now in true faith to Him who died for us, and believing on Him receive new life that will, by God's grace, produce fruit for Him.

Chapter 6

THE TONGUE TEST

IN THE FIRST TWO CHAPTERS of his epistle, James speaks of outward actions as indicating the faith (or lack of faith) in the heart. Words mean little if insincere. Perhaps some, however, because of his emphasis on *deeds,* might be led to think that it does not make any difference what we *say.* Not so, says James, and he proceeds to show in the opening verses of chapter 3 that words as well as actions are important, and in the final analysis lack of faith is shown not only by what people do, but also by what they say.

The first striking truth that he presents is the fact that *it is harder to control the tongue than the actions.* "My brethren, be not many masters, knowing that we shall receive the greater condemnation. For in many things we offend all. If any man offend not in word, the same is a perfect man, and able also to bridle the whole body" (vv. 1, 2).

A Word of Warning

The opening word is one of warning that we who are God's children should not aspire to be "many masters," or literally, "many teachers." Perhaps Calvin is right when he says: "The common and almost universal interpretation of this passage is, that the apostle discourages the desire for the office of teaching, and for this reason, because it is dangerous, and exposes one to a heavier judgment in case he transgresses; and they think that he said, 'Be not many masters,' because there ought to have been some. But I take masters not to be those who performed a public duty in the church, but such as took upon them the right of passing judgment upon others, for such reprovers sought to be accounted as masters of morals."

James is therefore warning us against having censorious or critical tongues that are always seeking to set other people right. This is not a manifestation of true faith—to be always criticizing others—but rather of "dead faith," for oftentimes people criticize others for the very things of which they themselves are guilty.

David bitterly condemned a rich man who had stolen the pet lamb of a poor neighbor, but apparently up to that time he had thought noth-

ing of his own sin of stealing his neighbor's wife
and murdering the husband (II Sam. 12).
"Therefore thou art inexcusable, O man, whosoever thou art that judgest: for wherein thou
judgest another, thou condemnest thyself; for
thou that judgest doest the same things" (Rom.
2:1).

Let us not be so quick to judge others and to
tell other people what *they* ought to do, for if
we do this, James says, "we shall receive the
greater condemnation [or judgment]." These
words are very similar to those of our blessed
Lord Himself when He said: "Judge not, that
ye be not judged" (Matt. 7:1). When we attempt to judge others, we are setting ourselves
up as those who have great light on such matters, and God will hold us responsible for that
light in relation to our own lives.

The reason we ought to be especially careful
about this matter, James says, is because "in
many things we offend all." This is not just a
matter of offending a few "touchy" people.
Some are so sensitive that it is impossible not to
offend them sooner or later, no matter what one
may do. James' allusion is not to this, but to the
fact that there are many obvious sins and failures
in the lives of each of us which are manifest to
all around us. How then can any individual

afford to set himself up as a judge of others when he himself is so full of imperfections? The old proverb puts it thus: "People that live in glass houses shouldn't throw stones."

As a matter of fact, we not only constantly commit offense in the things we do, but also in the things we *say;* so much so that James can truly write: "If any man offend not in word. the same is a perfect man, and able also to bridle the whole body." Yes, the tongue, though small, is harder to control than the whole body; if any of us were able to control it perfectly, then we could easily control the rest of our bodies.

SMALL BUT MIGHTY

But some may say, "The tongue is such a small thing, surely it is not difficult to control." James answers that *the size of things does not always indicate their importance.* "Behold, we put bits in the horses' mouths, that they may obey us; and we turn about their whole body. Behold also the ships, which though they be so great, and are driven of fierce winds, yet are they turned about with a very small helm, whithersoever the governor listeth. Even so the tongue is a little member, and boasteth great things" (vv. 3-5a).

Very important things are sometimes small in size. James illustrates this by speaking of the horse, and the ship. By means of a small bit placed in the mouth of the horse, we are able to turn his whole body. In like manner by using a helm, or rudder, small though it may be, we can direct the course of a ship. The comparison is drawn in the statement that "even so the tongue is a little member, and boasteth great things." In other words, the tongue claims great power for itself, and rightly so, for the whole passage shows that the tongue, though small, is very powerful and can cause great trouble if not properly controlled. How true it is that the tongue, like the rein or rudder, needs guidance itself!

Indeed we are told that *the untamed tongue defiles the whole body*. "Behold, how great a matter a little fire kindleth! And the tongue is a fire, a world of iniquity: so is the tongue among our members, that it defileth the whole body, and setteth on fire the course of nature; and is set on fire of hell. For every kind of beasts, and of birds, and of serpents, and of things in the sea, is tamed, and hath been tamed of mankind: but the tongue can no man tame; it is an unruly evil, full of deadly poison" (vv. 5b-8).

The thought of the importance of little things is continued with reference to "how great a matter [or wood] a little fire kindleth!" In one city a hot iron left on an ironing board started a fire that ended with the destruction of sixty city blocks, and the loss of millions of dollars' worth of property. And what a great strife has been occasioned sometimes by the tongue simply through the use of a few harsh words.

So it is easy to see why James goes on to describe the tongue as "a fire, a world of iniquity." It may be a little piece of flesh, and yet latent within it is a tremendous amount of evil, "a world of iniquity." It defiles the whole body: "Foul speech, heard in schools or places of business, read in filthy books, heard in theatres, has polluted many a young life, and kindled fires which have destroyed a man, body and soul" (Alexander Maclaren).

Satanic Fire

Further, it "sets on fire the course of nature [or *the cycle of creation*]." The affairs of all mankind are sometimes thrown into confusion by the rash, ungodly use of the tongue. And the tongue itself is "set on fire of hell." Behind much of this evil talk is Satan himself as he tempts and seeks to lead us into sin through the unwise use of the tongue.

For another graphic illustration, James turns to the wild beasts of the earth. Though many of these wild animals are ferocious and deadly, yet men have tamed even the worst by long and patient labor. But the tongue, we are told, is worse than any of these—it is an unruly evil and full of poison more deadly than that of a serpent: "no *man* can tame it."

Here again is something that *we* cannot handle by our own efforts alone. Note the emphasis on the word *man*. Though no *man* can tame the tongue, thank God there is One who can do so. The same Lord to whom the Psalmist long ago prayed can indeed make not only "the words of my mouth," but also "the meditations of my heart" acceptable in His sight (Ps. 19:14). Do you know this One as your Lord and Saviour?

Finally, James indicates that *an inconsistent life is revealed by the tongue.* "Therewith bless we God, even the Father; and therewith curse we men, which are made after the similitude of God. Out of the same mouth proceedeth blessing and cursing. My brethren, these things ought not so to be. Doth a fountain send forth at the same place sweet water and bitter? Can the fig tree, my brethren, bear olive berries? either a vine, figs? so can no fountain both yield salt water and fresh" (vv. 9-12).

What strange and paradoxical words are found on the tongues of men! James pictures a mouth that is uttering at one moment words of religious devotion to God, and yet a little later is cursing fellow men—men, remember, who are made "after the similitude of God."

Man in the beginning was made in the image of God. True, much of this image was lost in the Fall, but some of it yet appears. Remember that Absalom of old, though fallen into sin, still bore in his person a resemblance to his great father. So if we truly love God and mean our words of praise to Him, then we will demonstrate it by love for our fellow men, by speaking words of kindness and blessing rather than words of cursing.

The ordinarily gentle apostle John is very strong on this point. He says: "If a man say, I love God, and hateth his brother, he is a liar: for he that loveth not his brother whom he hath seen, how can he love God whom he hath not seen?" (I John 4:20).

Certainly we can all understand that it is inconsistent for blessing and cursing to proceed from the same mouth—just as incongruous as to imagine that a fountain can send forth both bitter and sweet water at the same time, or that a fig tree can produce olive berries, or a vine produce figs. "The 'cursing' destroys the reality of the verbal 'blessing God.' If a man says both, the imprecation is his genuine voice, and the other is mere wind" (Maclaren). No, each thing is going to produce fruit according to its nature, and evil speech on the tongue gives evidence that it is the fruit of an unregenerate nature that knows not God.

Remember, as indicated earlier, that no man can tame the tongue, but there is One who can. Bitter waters were made sweet at Marah when a divinely revealed tree was cast into them (Exod. 15:23-26). So as *the tree*—the cross of Christ—becomes real in our lives, as we trust in the Lord Jesus and walk in faith with Him, the bitter waters of Marah will become sweet, and our tongues instead of producing evil will be a blessing to all about us.

Chapter 7

EARTHLY AND HEAVENLY WISDOM

Wisdom, according to Scripture revelation, is one of the most desirable things in life. "For wisdom is better than rubies; and all the things that may be desired are not to be compared to it" (Prov. 8:11).

In this connection the terms *knowledge* and *wisdom* should be carefully distinguished. *Knowledge* refers to the possession of facts; *wisdom*, according to *Webster's Dictionary*, refers to the ability "to judge soundly and deal sagaciously with facts, especially as they relate to life and conduct." Some men possess a great deal of *knowledge* but very little *wisdom*, while there are others whose *knowledge* may not be extensive but who use the facts they do possess very wisely.

In the last portion of the third chapter of his epistle (vv. 13-18) James reveals to us that there are two kinds of wisdom in this world: *earthly wisdom* that is mere cunning and craft, and *heavenly wisdom* that comes from God. Those who have real faith in God should strive to attain this heavenly wisdom.

MATCH WORDS WITH WORKS

First we are told that true wisdom is shown by a good life: "Who is a wise man and endued with knowledge among you? let him show out of good conversation his works with meekness of wisdom" (v. 13).

Observe that James once more introduces his subject by asking a question. He asks: "Who is a wise man and endued with knowledge among you?" He does not mean to imply by this question that there are none among his readers who are truly wise, but rather he is challenging those who make great profession with the tongue, those who set themselves up as judges and censors of others, those who boast of their faith and wisdom, to match their words with their actions.

Someone has well said, "Many wish to appear wise, few really are." James indicates that a truly wise man is one who has a good store of knowledge (he is "endued with knowledge"—he seeks the true facts about things), but that is not all. He puts those facts into practical use in his life. So we are told that anyone who claims to be wise should "show out of good conversation his works with meekness of wisdom."

Carefully observe the word *show*. This takes us once again to the thought of James 2:18 ("I will *show* thee my faith by my works"), and again strikes the keynote of the entire epistle. If we truly have faith, we will *show* it by our outward actions, by our good works. If we have true wisdom, we will *show* it by the way we act in our daily lives.

It should be particularly noted that the word *conversation,* as used at the time our Authorized Version of the Bible was translated, had a far greater breadth of meaning than it now usually has. We limit the word to the talk that comes forth from our lips. The Greek word from which this is translated means in its literal form "a turning up and down," that is, life is considered as a quick motion to and fro. Thus it refers to the way we "turn up and down" through all of life—not only to our speech, but to all our conduct. So James is telling us that wisdom and knowledge, like faith, are dead, unless they produce good behavior.

WORKS WITH INWROUGHT MEEKNESS

But let us pursue the thought of the writer a bit farther. We are to show our wisdom by good works produced in our daily behavior, but this is to be done not in a sanctimonious or phari-saical manner, but "with meekness."

How little is this grace of *meekness* shown today by those who are seeking to serve God! The Scripture tells us that this virtue was pecu-liarly manifested in the life of our blessed Sa-viour, the One who said: "I am meek and lowly in heart" (Matt. 11:29). Our Lord Jesus, the ideal and perfect man (as well as the divine Son of God), demonstrated the graces of meekness and humility to perfection.

As Archbishop Trench points out: "The scrip-tural *meekness* is not in a man's outward be-havior only; nor yet in his relations to his fellowmen; and little in his mere natural dispo-sition. Rather it is an inwrought grace of the soul; and the exercises of it are first and chiefly toward God (Matt. 11:29; Jas. 1:21). It is that temper of spirit in which we accept His dealings with us as good, and therefore without dis-puting or resisting; and it is closely linked with *humility,* and follows upon it (Eph. 4:2; Col. 3:12; cf. Zeph. 3:12); because it is only the humble heart which is also the meek; and which, as such, does not fight against God, and more or less struggle and contend with Him.

"This meekness, however, being first of all a meekness before God, is also such in the face of men, even of evil men, out of a sense that these, with the insults and injuries which they may inflict, are permitted and employed by Him for the chastening and purifying of His elect. This was the root of David's meekness, when Shimei cursed and flung stones at him — the consideration, namely, that the Lord had bidden him (II Sam. 16:11), that it was just for him to suffer these things, however unjustly the other might inflict them; and out of like convictions all true Christian meekness must spring. He that is meek indeed will know himself as a sinner among sinners, or, if there was One who could not know Himself such, yet He too bore a sinner's doom, and endured therefore the contradiction of sinners (Luke 23:35, 36; John 18:22, 23)—and this knowledge of his own sin will teach him to endure meekly the provocations with which they may provoke him, and not to withdraw himself from the burdens which their sin may impose upon him (Gal. 6:1; II Tim. 2:25; Titus 3:2)."

We should never confuse *meekness* with *weakness.* The words sound alike, but are quite different. True meekness should ever characterize those who have true wisdom—let us do that which is good and right, but do it with modesty, with gentleness, with courtesy, with patience, with mildness, with godly moderation. For practical examples of wisdom and meekness, one has merely to read of the lives of such godly men as Lincoln in America and Gladstone in England. But remember, that which James speaks of here is not a natural quality of fallen man, but a fruit of the indwelling Spirit of God (Gal. 5:22,23).

EARTHLY VS. HEAVENLY WISDOM

Next James turns to a comparison of earthly and heavenly wisdom. First he deals with *earthly wisdom and its result.* "But if ye have bitter envying and strife in your hearts, glory not, and lie not against the truth. This wisdom descendeth not from above, but is earthly, sensual, devilish. For where envying and strife is, there is confusion and every evil work" (vv. 14-16).

Note the words *but if ye have.* The implication in the Greek is that this is true. James is observant that there is contentiousness in some who are claiming great things with regard to faith and wisdom, so he says, "If ye have bitter envying and strife in your hearts, glory not."

Two things are here mentioned: *bitter envying* and *strife,* or (as recently revised) *bitter jealousy* and *selfish ambition.* Oh, how many of us who claim to believe God's Word and consider that we have the true wisdom could well have these words used to characterize our lives!

Our hearts are filled with envy and jealousy of others, and that of the bitterest type.

Envy is always pictured in the Bible as the very worst of passions. What is *envy?* To begrudge others their success. Someone else makes a more conspicuous success in some field than we do, and instead of rejoicing over the way that person is being used of the Lord, our hearts are filled with bitter jealousy.

Oh, my brethren, such things ought not to be! Read what the apostle Paul says in I Corinthians 12:12-27. Do not glory over your wisdom if bitter jealousy is in your heart, for this is not a manifestation of heavenly *wisdom.*

The other thing is *strife* (or selfish ambition)— a reference to rivalry or a narrow party spirit. This is shown when the desire of the heart is not to glorify God, but to advance one's own selfish interests or that of some little clique with which he is identified. James not only warns against letting such things crop out in your actions, but he says if you have them "in your hearts, glory not." From the heart flows the deeds of the life, and if this sort of evil thing is in your heart, then sooner or later it will come out in full view. If such things are present in your heart, "glory not"—rather fall on your face before God, confess your sin, and ask Him to purify your inmost life and remove these evil vipers of passion.

James also says, "Lie not against the truth." How can a person *lie against the truth?* Simply thus: by living a life that does not agree with God's truth. No, says our writer, "this wisdom descendeth not from above." What wisdom is he talking about? Why, the supposed wisdom that can glory in envy, strife, bitterness, and impurity of life.

Old Matthew Henry has well said:

"Pretend what you will, and think yourself ever so wise, yet you have abundance of reason to cease your glorying, if you run down love and peace, and give way to bitter envying and strife. Your zeal for truth or orthodoxy, and your boasts of knowing more than others, if you employ these only to make others hateful, and to show your own spite and heart-burnings against them, are a shame to your profession of Christianity, and a downright contradiction to it. Lie not thus against the truth."

Such wisdom cannot be from God, who only gives good things (Jas. 1:17). On the contrary, wisdom of this kind is stated to be *earthly, sensual, devilish.* It is *earthly* in that it comes not from Heaven, not from God, but from corrupt, fallen human nature as found on this earth, which in reality is opposed to God and good.

This envious, warlike wisdom is also said to be *sensual*. It comes purely from the human senses, an animal-like thing; it comes from the *natural* man—the natural man, of course, referring to man in the natural state in which he is born as a sinful, fallen creature who has not experienced the regenerating work of God's Holy Spirit.

But even worse, this earthly wisdom James is talking about is also said to be *devilish*. It originates not from God, but from the devil himself, that great enemy of God. Erdman has truly said: "It may be employed in discussing religious truth, it may be displayed in defending 'orthodoxy,' but it is evidently not inspired by the Spirit of God; no matter what his intellectual attainments no one should pride himself upon a wisdom which is so closely allied with 'the world, the flesh, and the devil.'"

What is the result of such wisdom? "For where envying and strife is, there is confusion and every evil work." Once again Jemes refers to envying and the strife which results from it. What a terrible thing envy is! "The envious man stands in his own light. He thinks his candle cannot shine in the presence of another's sun.

He aims directly at man, obliquely at God, who makes men to differ" (Alford).

The result of such an attitude is *confusion*— literally, *tumultuous anarchy,* or commotion, both in society as a whole, and in the mind of the individual who harbors such thoughts. Beyond confusion and disorder, there will be "every evil deed" or "every vile practice" (A.R.V.); for when men allow their hearts to be filled with jealousy and selfish ambition, they will stoop to "every vile practice" in order to further their own ends.

Fruits of Heavenly Wisdom

But now we turn from the dark, dismal valley to the bright, glorious mountain peak, from *earthly* to *heavenly wisdom.* "But the wisdom that is from above is first pure, then peaceable, gentle, and easy to be entreated, full of mercy and good fruits, without partiality, and without hypocrisy. And the fruit of righteousness is sown in peace of them that make peace" (vv. 17, 18).

Seven fruits of *heavenly wisdom* are itemized. If a person is truly wise, they are the ways in which such wisdom will be demonstrated.

Heavenly wisdom is "first pure." It should be carefully observed that *purity* is placed before *peace.* There are occasions when both *peace* and *purity* cannot be preserved (Rom. 12:18). If both cannot be maintained, then purity must come first. "Peace at any price" is not the teaching of God's Word, either with regard to the world or to the Church.

Sometimes when faithful men of God seek to correct evil practices which may be present in the Church, they are told that they themselves are doing evil in that they are "disturbing the peace of the Church." Ordination services usually contain a question something like this: "Do you promise to be zealous and faithful in maintaining the truths of the gospel and the *purity* and *peace* of the Church, whatever persecution or opposition may arise unto you on that account?" (*Presbyterian Book of Church Order*). Here again is the scriptural sequence: first purity, then peace. An older writer has truly said: "There is an unholy peace with the world that makes no distinction between clean and unclean. Our first concern should be purity."

But remember that after purity, the second characteristic of true wisdom is that it is *peaceable* and *gentle.* Instead of harshly criticizing others and judging them, it is forebearing, making allowances for others as to their duty which they owe us. Further, it is *easy to be entreated,* not harsh with the faults of others. Many earnest Christians instead of "restoring" those "overtaken in a fault . . . in the spirit of meekness" (Gal. 6:1) are stern and legalistic in their attitude toward the failures of others. They are not "easy to be entreated."

True wisdom is also said to be *full* (or overflowing) with *mercy and good fruits.* In addition, it is *without partiality,* a matter which James has already discussed at some length in chapter 2.

Finally, it is *without hypocrisy.* There is no sham or dissimulation with the person who is truly wise. He is not pretending to be something he is not, as in the case of many of the Pharisees. They pretended to be very religious, but only, as our Lord Jesus stated, in order that they might have cloak for their evil deeds.

James closes the section with a reminder of a very important fact: "And the fruit of righteousness is sown in peace of them that make peace." If we are going to *reap* the fruit of righteousness in peace, there must first be a *sowing* of such fruit in the life. Weymouth translates the verse thus: "And righteousness is the fruit of the seed that is sown in peace by the peacemakers." If we truly have heavenly wisdom we will be *peacemakers.*

Calvin has well said: "Those who wish to be the physicians to heal vices ought not to be the executioners." So let those who are Christians remember that we are not called to be *executioners* of sinners, but rather the *physicians*, showing them by our words and our manner of life the way in which they too can know the healing, saving power of Christ.

Chapter 8

THE CAUSE AND CURE OF UNREST

As we survey the history of humanity, we find it full of bloodshed and violence, wars and fightings, tumult and strife. This brings to our attention very forcibly the sad but true fact that the world is full of unregenerated men. Everywhere hearts are filled with unrest. Unfortunately many Christians carry over some of the restlessness inherent in natural man into their new life.

In the opening verses of James 4 we find the secret of the cause and cure of unrest.

In verses 1-4 James discloses the *cause*. First of all, he says it is due to *lustfulness*. "From whence come wars and fightings among you? come they not hence, even of your lusts that war in your members? Ye lust, and have not: ye kill, and desire to have, and cannot obtain: ye fight and war, yet ye have not, because ye ask not. Ye ask, and receive not, because ye ask amiss, that ye may consume it upon your lusts" (vv. 1-3).

How striking is the contrast between the first verse of chapter 4 and the last verse of chapter 3! In the latter verse *peace* is mentioned no less than twice as being the outcome of heavenly wisdom. But in the very next verse *war* is mentioned twice and fightings once.

People of our generation have unceasingly asked, "How can wars be stopped?" "How can we rid the earth permanently of war?" James probes deeper. He asks: "From whence come wars and fightings among you?" Before the answer can be found to the question of how we can *dispose* of war, we must solve this deeper problem of the *cause* of wars and fightings.

The answer is given in the same verse in the form of another question: "Come they not hence, even of your lusts that war in your members?" So wars and fightings start not on the *outside*, but on the *inside* of men. The origin is said to be *lustfulness*. There are lusts within the hearts of men which war within the very members of the body. These lusts flow through the individual, and from thence to society at large.

SEED OF UNREST

What are lusts? Simply *evil desires*. Desire is not bad in itself; but when we desire that which is not ours, that which it is not lawful for us to have, then that is evil—*lust*.

It is probable that James is speaking here primarily of contentions between professing Christians, since he speaks of "you" and he is writing to those who call themselves believers in Christ. At the same time the fact he brings out is true whether in the Church or in the world at large. As long as there are evil lusts unrestrained within the hearts of human beings, these lusts are going to manifest themselves continually in wars and fightings.

And the supreme tragedy of it all is that although men will go to any extreme to satisfy these evil passions, yet in the end they remain *unsatisfied*. "Ye lust, and have not: ye kill, and desire to have, and cannot obtain: ye fight and war, yet ye have not because ye ask not."

Observe the steps downward—first there is the passionate, but unfulfilled, desire in the heart. (The word *lust* as used here represents a different Greek word from that of verse 1, and signifies "to set one's mind or heart on an object.") Then to fulfill the evil desire on

which one has set his heart, he turns to outward
action to envy, killing, and war.

Perhaps some may say: "Surely this could
not apply to me, for I would never kill." Such
should remember I John 3:15: "Whosoever
hateth his brother is a murderer." There can
also be a very literal application, for it is possible for a person through envy and evil desire
actually to kill another—witness David's ap-
palling crime.

Striving and Asking

But notice the sad conclusion: even after all
this bitter strife and envying, this stooping to
any means to get the thing desired, in the end
the heart remains unsatisfied and still filled with
unrest—"yet ye have not." Oh, how foolish to
strive in this way for the wind, when our heavenly Father has promised to give us all the good
things we need to satisfy our hearts if we will
but ask Him!

So James says the reason we do not have that
which we need to bring real heart satisfaction
is not because we do not strive hard enough, but
simply because we do not come to this heavenly
Father in prayer and claim the promise: "Ask
and it shall be given." "Ye have not because
ye ask not." One of the older commentators

has well said: "God promises to those who pray, not to those who fight."

Immediately, however, someone raises an objection: "I asked but I did not receive the answer." In verse 3 James answers such an objection by saying, "Ye ask, and receive not, because ye ask amiss, that ye may consume it upon your lusts." The chief reason we lack the things we need is that we simply do not take the time to come and ask God for them.

But when we do pray, God many times does not give us the thing we ask for, because we ask not for that which is for His glory and our real good, but rather for that which we want simply to satisfy our own selfish passions. Remember the words of the apostle John: "And this is the confidence that we have in him, that, if we ask anything *according to his will,* he heareth us: and if we know that he hear us, whatsoever we ask, we know that we have the petitions that we desired of him" (I John 5:14, 15). Like pampered, spoiled children we whine to God for things that would harm rather than help us, and out of love to us He cannot give the answer to such prayers.

Beyond this, James tells us that this unrest comes not only from *lustfulness,* but also from *worldly-mindedness.* "Ye adulterers and adulteresses, know ye not that the friendship of the world is enmity with God? whosoever therefore will be a friend of the world is the enemy of God" (v. 4). In the original text the term "adulterers and adulteresses" is only one word: "Ye adulteresses." The word is here used in a spiritual sense. When those who name the name of Christ are unfaithful to Him, they are *spiritual adulteresses* (the word is properly used in the feminine form since the Church is the *Bride* of Christ).

You cannot walk in spiritual fellowship with God and at the same time with the ungodly evil world. "Love not the world, neither the things that are in the world. If any man love the world, the love of the Father is not in him. For all that is in the world, the lust of the flesh, and the lust of the eyes, and the pride of life, is not of the Father, but is of the world. And the world passeth away, and the lust thereof: but he that doeth the will of God abideth forever" (I John 2:15-17).

There must be a choice: which do you want—God, or this cosmos world? Isaac Watts, in one of his grand old hymns, asks this significant question: "Is this vile world a friend to grace to help me on to God?"